Note to parents, carers and teachers

Read it yourself is a series of modern stories, favourite characters and traditional tales written in a simple way for children who are learning to read. The books can be read independently or as part of a guided reading session.

Each book is carefully structured to include many high-frequency words vital for first reading. The sentences on each page are supported closely by pictures to help with understanding, and to offer lively details to talk about.

The books are graded into four levels that progressively introduce wider vocabulary and longer stories as a reader's ability and confidence grows.

Ideas for use

- Begin by looking through the book and talking about the pictures. Has your child heard this story before?

- Help your child with any words he does not know, either by helping him to sound them out or supplying them yourself.

- Developing readers can be concentrating so hard on the words that they sometimes don't fully grasp the meaning of what they're reading. Answering the puzzle questions at the end of the book will help with understanding.

For more information and advice on Read it yourself and book banding, visit **www.ladybird.com/readityourself**

Book
Band
7

Level 2 is ideal for children who have received some reading instruction and can read short, simple sentences with help.

Special features:

Frequent repetition of main story words and phrases

Short, simple sentences

Peppa and her friends are going on a school bus trip.

"Is everyone here?" says Madame Gazelle.

"Yes," they say.

Everyone loves school trips.

6

7

Large, clear type

"Where are we going for our trip?" says Peppa.

"We are going to the mountains," says Madame Gazelle.

"Hooray!" everyone says. They all look out as they go.

Careful match between story and pictures

8

9

Educational Consultant: Geraldine Taylor
Book Banding Consultant: Kate Ruttle

LADYBIRD BOOKS

UK | USA | Canada | Ireland | Australia
India | New Zealand | South Africa

Ladybird Books is part of the Penguin Random House group of companies
whose addresses can be found at global.penguinrandomhouse.com.

www.penguin.co.uk   www.puffin.co.uk   www.ladybird.co.uk

Penguin
Random House
UK

Text adapted from School Bus Trip, first published by Ladybird Books, 2008
This version first published by Ladybird Books, 2014
012

This book is based on the
TV Series 'Peppa Pig'
'Peppa Pig' is created by
Neville Astley and Mark Baker
Peppa Pig © Astley Baker Davies Ltd/
Entertainment One UK Ltd, 2003

www.peppapig.com

Printed in China

A CIP catalogue record for this book is
available from the British Library

ISBN: 978-0-723-28087-3

MIX
Paper from
responsible sources
FSC® C018179

School Bus Trip

Adaptation written by Ellen Philpott
Based on the TV series 'Peppa Pig'. 'Peppa Pig' is created
by Neville Astley and Mark Baker

Peppa and her friends are going on a school bus trip.

"Is everyone here?" says Madame Gazelle.

"Yes," they say.

Everyone loves school trips.

7

"Where are we going for our trip?" says Peppa.

"We are going to the mountains," says Madame Gazelle.

"Hooray!" everyone says. They all look out as they go.

9

The bus is going to the top of a big mountain. It is very high up.

"Come on, bus!" says Peppa.

Up, up, up they go.

The children sing a song as they go.

The bus gets to the top
and everyone gets out.

"Come and look at the
big mountains," says
Madame Gazelle.

Peppa looks at the mountains. She is very high up.

"Wow," she says.

Everyone hears, "Wow, wow, wow."

wow wow

15

"What was that?"
says Peppa.

"That was an echo," says
Madame Gazelle. "It is what
you hear when you call out,
up in the mountains."

"Come on, everyone," says Peppa. "We can all make an echo."

The children call out, "Wow." They can hear, "Wow, wow, wow."

Everyone loves echoes.

WOW WOW WOW

WOW

"Come on, children," says Madame Gazelle. "It is time for our picnic."

"Hooray," says everyone.

"Where are the ducks?" says Peppa. "They love it when we have picnics, too."

Peppa and her friends look out for the ducks.

Here come the ducks.

"Hooray," says Peppa.

"Quack, quack, quack," say the ducks.

"Come here, ducks,"
says Madame Gazelle.

"Yes, come to our
picnic, ducks," says Peppa.

Then the ducks have a
big picnic, too.

It is time to go back to
school. The children get
in the bus. Then they sing
a song as they go back
down the mountain.

Everyone loves
school trips.

How much do you remember about Peppa Pig: School Bus Trip? Answer these questions and find out!

- Where are Peppa and her friends going?

- What do the children do on the bus?

- What does everyone hear when Peppa says, "Wow"?

- Which animals come to the picnic?

Look at the pictures and match them to the story words.

mountain

bus

picnic

ducks

Madame Gazelle

Read it yourself with Ladybird

Tick the books you've read!

For beginner readers who can read short, simple sentences with help.

For more confident readers who can read simple stories with help.